A Day With A
NOBLEWOMAN

A Day With A
Noblewoman

by Régine Pernoud

Illustrations by Giorgio Bacchin
Translated by Dominique Clift

RP

Runestone Press/Minneapolis
A Division of the Lerner Publishing Group

All words that appear in **bold** are explained in the
glossary that starts on page 43.

This edition first published in the United States in 1997 by Runestone Press.

Runestone Press, c/o The Lerner Publishing Group
241 First Avenue North, Minneapolis, MN 55401 U.S.A.

Additional artwork by Tiziano Murgia, pp. 8 (map), 11 (map), 12–13 (map),
14 (bottom), 15 (bottom); Giacinto Guadenzi, pp. 9, 10 (top), 12 (top), 14 (top),
15 (top); Remo Berselli, p. 13 (top).

Library of Congress Cataloging-in-Publication Data

Pernoud, Régine.
[Una castellana. English]
A noblewoman / by Régine Pernoud ; illustrated by Giorgio
Bacchin; translated by Dominique Clift. — 1st American ed.
p.   cm.   —(A day with—)
Includes bibliographical references and index.
Summary: Summary: Describes, both factually and fictionally, the life of
Blanche of Navarre, countess of Champagne in thirteenth-century
France.
ISBN 0-8225-1916-X (lib. bdg. : alk. paper)
1. France—Civilization—1000-1328-Juvenile literature.
2. Women—France—Social life and customs—Juvenile literature.
3. Blanche, de Navarre, comtesse de Champagne, d. 1229—Juvenile
literature. 4. Nobility—France—Champagne—Biography—Juvenile
literature. I. Bacchin, Giorgio, ill. II. Title. III. Series.
DC33.2.P4313 1997
944'02.—dc21   96-47107
Manufactured in the United States of America
1 2 3 4 5 6 – JR – 02 01 00 99 98 97

CONTENTS

INTRODUCTION

Middle Ages and *medieval* are terms that refer to a period in European history. This period, which lasted from roughly A.D. 500 to A.D. 1500, is sandwiched between the Roman Empire and the **Renaissance,** or rebirth of interest in classical Greece and Rome. The ideas that took root during the Renaissance mark the beginning of the modern era of Europe's history.

During the Middle Ages, the lives of the people of Europe were centered around two important factors—the power of the **Roman Catholic Church** and the power of the **landowners.** These two factors shaped European society.

The Catholic Church, in addition to taking care of religious matters, offered opportunities for education, fostered the arts (such as music and sculpture), and supported massive building projects. People at every level of medieval life held strongly to Christian beliefs, and the decorations on churches were symbols of this faith and devotion.

The landowners—usually noble lords who lived in castles—held power under a governing system known as **feudalism.** Although a lord might owe loyalty to a king, within his own territory, he managed agriculture, trade, and industry. He collected taxes, demanded military service, and made judicial decisions.

Most ordinary people, known as **peasants,** lived and worked on the lord's land and had few rights. They tilled his soil, cut his wood, repaired his buildings—in short they did whatever the lord asked of them. In return, the lord used his knights to provide peace and security.

Some common folk, mainly merchants and **artisans,** were residents of towns. By about the eleventh century— the beginning of the **High Middle Ages**—Europe had many towns and several large cities. The first towns had been set up near castles, but increases in local trade had caused towns to develop along rivers and other commercial routes. Peasants began to leave rural areas to find jobs in towns. Craftworkers, merchants, food vendors, and innkeepers made up the towns' populations. Some peasants farmed their own land outside the towns and provided the townspeople with food.

This story about a medieval noblewoman takes place during the High Middle Ages in a county of northeastern France called Champagne. Blanche, the countess of Champagne, was originally from Navarre, a kingdom that lay partly in present-day France and partly in present-day Spain. Widowed within a few years of her marriage to the count of Champagne, she ably managed her son's estate until he was old enough to run it himself. Her duties varied widely from ensuring the safety of traveling merchants to repairing roads to attending important fairs.

Series Editors

PART ONE

THE WORLD OF A MEDIEVAL NOBLEWOMAN

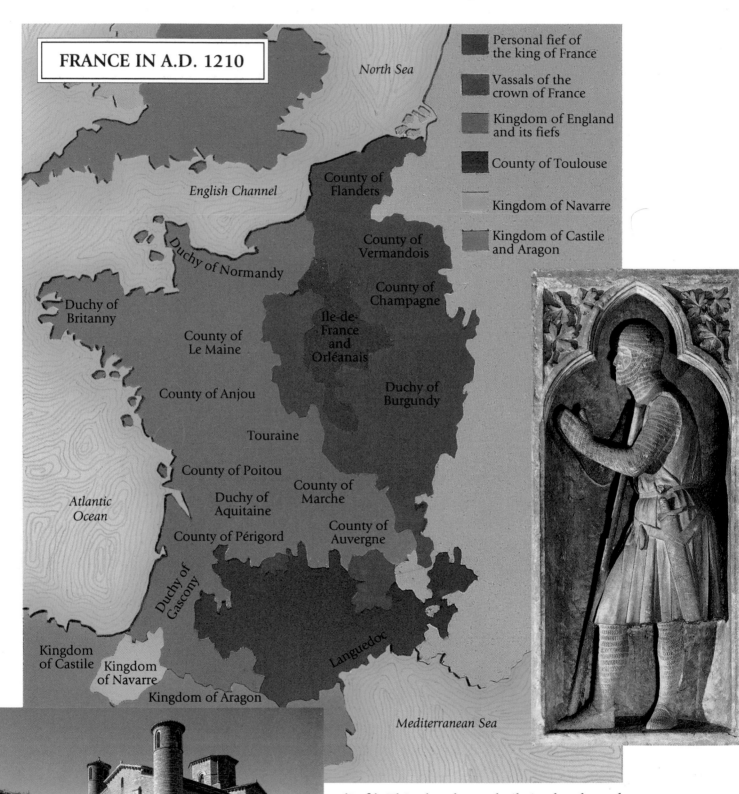

FRANCE IN A.D. 1210

Legend:
- Personal fief of the king of France
- Vassals of the crown of France
- Kingdom of England and its fiefs
- County of Toulouse
- Kingdom of Navarre
- Kingdom of Castile and Aragon

North Sea

English Channel

County of Flanders

County of Vermandois

County of Champagne

Duchy of Normandy

Île-de-France and Orléanais

Duchy of Britanny

County of Le Maine

County of Anjou

Duchy of Burgundy

Touraine

County of Poitou

County of Marche

Duchy of Aquitaine

Atlantic Ocean

County of Périgord

County of Auvergne

Duchy of Gascony

Languedoc

Kingdom of Castile

Kingdom of Navarre

Kingdom of Aragon

Mediterranean Sea

(Left) *This church was built in the eleventh century in the ancient kingdom of Navarre. This realm straddled the modern border between northern Spain and southwestern France. (Above) A statue from the* **cathedral** *in Reims—one of the important cities of Champagne—represents the biblical figure of Abraham as a medieval warrior.*

During the Middle Ages, France was made up of a number of **fiefs,** or feudal estates, that were administered by a lord or, occasionally, by a lady. The king, who also had his personal domain, settled conflicts that sometimes arose between the fiefdoms. A wide variety of people lived on these domains. The poorest folk were the **serfs,** who were bound by law to the lord's estate and who had few rights. Serfs could not leave the estate, nor could they be ejected from it.

(Above) *These illustrations of a farmer at work appear on a small painting, called a miniature, that dates from about 1280. In the Middle Ages, peasants were either freemen or serfs. A freeman was his own master, even though he gave a set amount of unpaid labor to the lord and was subject to taxation. The serf, on the other hand, worked without pay. Serfs could not choose their occupations, which were passed on from generation to generation. (Left) The drawing shows a noblewoman of a feudal estate keeping an eye on a load of merchandise. Her other responsibilities included resolving legal and public matters, managing the budget of the fief, and running a large household.*

The story that follows describes a day in the life of Blanche, the countess of Champagne. She was the daughter of King Sancho VI of Navarre and married Count Thibaut III of Champagne in 1199. Soon after their wedding, her husband "took the cross"— meaning he volunteered to fight in foreign religious wars known as the **Crusades.** He died in 1201, while traveling to the departure site for the Fourth Crusade. Suddenly widowed, Blanche was painstakingly attentive to the education of their son, Thibaut IV. Later known as the Songwriter, Thibaut IV was among the greatest poets of thirteenth-century France.

Blanche of Champagne was responsible for her son's vast domain. The county of Champagne, a flat, fertile land famous for its wines, was prosperous. Its

(Above) *An illustration shows the type of clothing worn by noblemen and noblewomen of France in the early thirteenth century.*

(Right) *In this fourteenth-century miniature, the bishop of Paris blesses a fair held every June near Paris. Some medieval fairs were so important that they required the presence of Roman Catholic authorities. Religious festivals were often held at the same time as the fairs.*

rivers, such as the Marne, the Aube, and the Seine, generated substantial commercial traffic. Champagne's chief cities—including Bar-sur-Aube, Troyes, Provins, and Lagny—hosted large fairs between January and September. Blanche was responsible for the maintenance of roads and bridges that passed through her domain. She also ensured the safety of the merchants traveling through her territory. Upon arriving in Provins, for example, merchants were allowed to store their goods in huge caves that had been cut into the chalky stone that lay beneath the city.

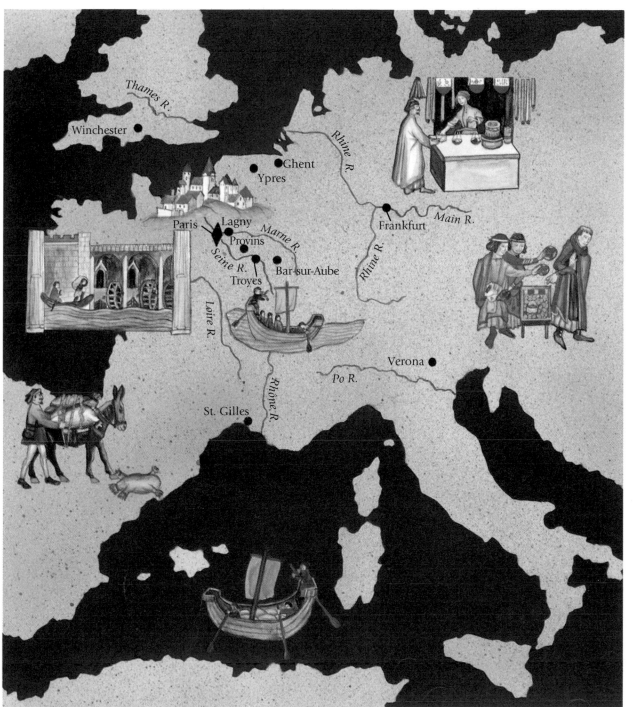

(Above) *Another miniature shows commercial activities that were typical of Champagne's fairs. The three merchants are arranging their wares —shoes, clothes, and gold and silver embroidery.*

(Left) *Dots locate the most important fairs of the 1200s. Merchants would often reach these cities using the main navigable waterways. The region east and southeast of Paris between the Marne and the Seine Rivers—in the ancient domain of Champagne—had the greatest number of events.*

(Left) Constantinople (modern Istanbul, Turkey) was the capital of the Byzantine Empire. The city was also one of the endpoints of the Silk Road. This ancient route began in the Chinese Empire, where precious fabrics were produced. Via caravan, the fabrics then made their way to the Byzantine Empire and the Mediterranean region. Constantinople's busy port became a major crossroads of trade between Asia and Europe.

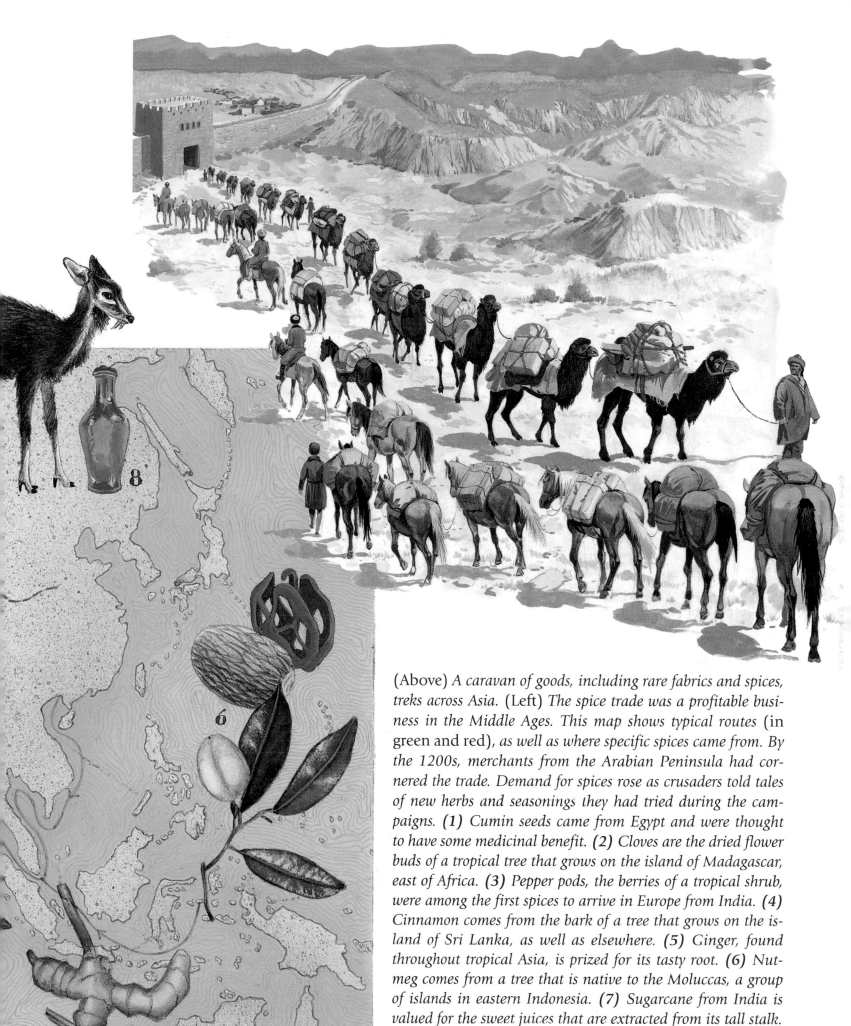

(Above) *A caravan of goods, including rare fabrics and spices, treks across Asia.* (Left) *The spice trade was a profitable business in the Middle Ages. This map shows typical routes (in green and red), as well as where specific spices came from. By the 1200s, merchants from the Arabian Peninsula had cornered the trade. Demand for spices rose as crusaders told tales of new herbs and seasonings they had tried during the campaigns.* **(1)** *Cumin seeds came from Egypt and were thought to have some medicinal benefit.* **(2)** *Cloves are the dried flower buds of a tropical tree that grows on the island of Madagascar, east of Africa.* **(3)** *Pepper pods, the berries of a tropical shrub, were among the first spices to arrive in Europe from India.* **(4)** *Cinnamon comes from the bark of a tree that grows on the island of Sri Lanka, as well as elsewhere.* **(5)** *Ginger, found throughout tropical Asia, is prized for its tasty root.* **(6)** *Nutmeg comes from a tree that is native to the Moluccas, a group of islands in eastern Indonesia.* **(7)** *Sugarcane from India is valued for the sweet juices that are extracted from its tall stalk.* **(8)** *Musk, a liquid used in perfumes, is obtained from the glands of a small hornless deer known as the musk deer.*

(Above) *By the thirteenth century, Champagne was already an important wine-producing area. In addition to growing and harvesting the grapes, serfs pressed the grapes and preserved the juice in wooden casks. Some peasants were skilled at making and repairing the wine barrels.* (Right) *This drawing is a modern artist's view of how Provins may have looked at the beginning of the thirteenth century. The castle, located in the high part of the city, included the Tower of Caesar. The Church of St. Ayoul (lower right), the main place of worship, was rebuilt on several occasions.*

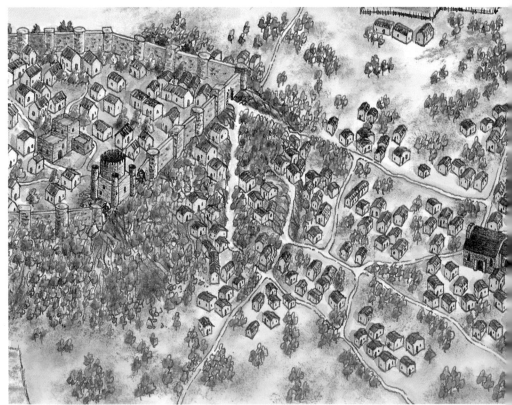

Thibaut IV of Champagne (1201–1253) was admired during his own time as well as in later centuries for his religious poems. Although a skilled composer, he was not a great political strategist. At one point, he joined a group that opposed his beloved cousin, Queen Blanche of Castile, the mother of young Louis IX of France and the country's **regent.** After Thibaut and the queen reconciled, she helped him avoid additional political pitfalls. Through his mother—the noblewoman in the story that follows—Thibaut inherited the kingdom of Navarre in 1234. One of Thibaut's descendants, Joan of Navarre, married Philip, who would later become the king of France. Because of this marriage, France was able to take over not only Champagne but also Navarre. Joan and Philip's male descendants were called the kings of France and Navarre, a title that survived for centuries.

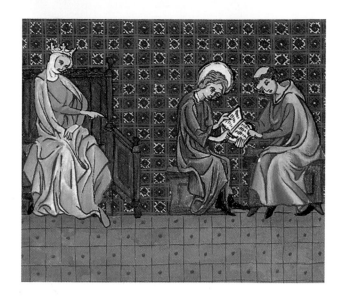

(Above) *In this miniature from a four-teenth-century manuscript, Queen Blanche of Castile supervises the education of her son Louis IX, who ruled France from 1226 to 1270. Blanche of Castile is the cousin and childhood friend of Thibaut IV, the youth featured in the story to follow.*

(Left) *The rose of Provins, a particular variety of red rose, had become the emblem of the English royal House of Lancaster by the fifteenth century. The House of York, Lancaster's rival, used a white rose as its symbol. The long conflict between these two houses over the kingship of England was known as the War of the Roses (1455–1485).*

The story that follows traces the daily activities of a real person—Blanche, the widowed countess of Champagne. Her husband, Thibaut III, died in 1201, just as he was about to leave on the Fourth Crusade. This foreign religious war would have taken him to the Holy Land, a region in the Middle East that is sacred to Christians, Jews, and Muslims (followers of the Islamic faith). During the Middle Ages, the Holy Land was in the hands of Arab and later Turkish Muslims. The Crusaders attempted but ultimately failed to wrest control of the Holy Land from these non-Christians.

Blanche of Champagne was pregnant with Thibaut IV when her husband died. Under the feudal system, each noble owed loyalty to someone higher in rank. Therefore, at his birth, the boy became a royal **ward** under the protection—and authority—of Philip Augustus, the king of France. Blanche worked hard to safeguard her son's inheritance from being absorbed by the king, who used wardships as a way of increasing his power as well as his income. As a royal ward, Thibaut IV was expected to spend time in the king's household.

Philip Augustus eyed the county of Champagne for good reason. It was a large, fertile, prosperous domain. The counts of Champagne held many fiefs in the region and had the sworn loyalty of many nobles of lesser rank. Merchants, attracted to Champagne's low taxes and safe highways, crisscrossed the county to go to its famous and well-attended fairs. Blanche, who managed the territory while her son was young, was responsible for maintaining its roads, bridges, and waterways. She built or renovated the county's castles and put her orders in writing to ensure that they were carried out. In fact, chroniclers of the time noted that Blanche, who died in 1229, showed a "manly side" in the strong way that she preserved and improved her son's inheritance.

PART TWO

A Day with Blanche, a Thirteenth-Century Noblewoman

Blanche, Countess of Champagne, was always up before sunrise. Her personal maid, Constance, had hoped that after yesterday's journey to the castle at Provins, the countess would sleep in. But Constance was to be disappointed. Blanche was already out of bed getting her clothes together. Constance couldn't help sighing as she got up. From the barnyard below came the sound of the cock crowing. Another exhausting day had begun. Blanche ignored the need to rest and set a busy pace for her household. A ray of sunshine broke between the curtains. It, too, was trained to follow her routine.

Blanche of Champagne was an energetic feudal ruler. The business of her domain hardly left her any time to relax. Her greatest comforts were prayer, music, and poetry. Already draped in her full-length dress, she was praying before her crucifix in preparation for Mass to be sung at the Church of St. Ayoul. Morning prayers were also a time for memories. Her first prayer was for her husband, who had died so young.

Blanche had been in her teens when she'd said farewell to her father, King Sancho VI, and her homeland of Navarre to marry Thibaut III, Count of Champagne. She'd left her native mountains in the southwest of France to live on the vast plains of Champagne in the northeast.

Life had seemed to smile on her and Thibaut. She'd first met her future husband during a trip to the Spanish kingdom of Aragon. When her father later told her about the count's formal request of marriage, she'd felt no hesitation in saying yes. Thibaut of Champagne was a remarkable dancer and a most friendly knight. The couple's trip across France had been festive, with the high point being their wedding in 1199 at the Cathedral of Sens at the edge of Champagne. Afterward they had toured the county's major cities, where she had been greeted with exceptional warmth.

A few months later, Blanche had attended a tournament that her husband had organized at Ecry-sur-Aisne, a city in the northern part of Champagne. Many knights from Champagne and from the nearby region of Flanders had been invited. Standards and pennants had waved in the wind on the tournament grounds. Viewing stands had overlooked the field where the combat and competitions were to take place.

The atmosphere at the tournament had reached a high pitch of excitement. So the spectators had been startled when, instead of the expected knights, a small man in a black robe had appeared on the field. He was Foulques, the priest in charge of the parish at Neuilly, near Paris. Before the hushed gathering, he had exhorted the knights to forsake their laughable combats and to offer their swords for the retaking of the Holy Land. Foulques had announced that Jerusalem, the Holy City, had recently fallen to the armies of the Muslim general Saladin. It was the duty of all Christians, he'd said, to go to the city's rescue.

Foulques of Neuilly was a fiery preacher whose words had drawn tears from his listeners. One after another, each knight had removed his colorful ceremonial apparel, exchanging it for the simple clothing of the Crusades—a white tunic bearing a red cross.

Remembering these circumstances, Blanche always felt the same emotion. She, too, had yearned to go to the Holy Land to face the same perils as her husband. But he had dissuaded her with just a few words—she was pregnant. This was not the time for her to go on a dangerous expedition or to suffer long days on horseback.

Only in her morning prayers did Blanche recall the events that had followed. The other nobles who had rallied to the cause had named Thibaut III head of the expedition. But he had been overwhelmed by a sudden fever and had died even before leaving French soil. Blanche had been left alone with the child she was expecting.

That had been 10 years ago. Since then, Blanche had refused to remarry so she could devote herself entirely to the education of her son, Thibaut IV. This morning her prayer was for the safety of this boy who had never known his father. A year ago, Thibaut had been sent to spend time at the court of Philip Augustus, the king of France, and her beloved son would soon be on his way home. What hopes he carried!

Constance came closer and with a little sign indicated that the bath she'd ordered the previous evening was ready. Two footmen had brought in a wooden tub lined with thick towels in which they had poured hot water. The towels protected the bather's skin from the tub's splinters. Behind a curtain, with the help of Constance and another woman working in the castle, Blanche washed and dried herself. She dressed for what she knew would be a very long day.

It was September 3, Saint Ayoul's Day. A little-known saint, Ayoul had been honored by a church built in his name in Provins. Each year on this day, the townspeople celebrated a solemn Mass for the beginning of the renowned fair of Provins. The fair was why the countess of Champagne had been so eager to return to her castle in Provins.

The church bells were pealing, calling together the people of Provins. Already the merchants and their potential customers were gathering. Mules and carts created huge traffic jams in the narrow streets of the walled city. Escorted by Constance, several footmen, a few **squires,** and other maids from the castle, Blanche headed for the church. The small group took the way that ran on top of the **ramparts.** From this vantage point, they could see the whole city and the surrounding countryside. The group took a steep street to the lower town where the Church of St. Ayoul stood.

The church's main entrance had three **portals.** Sculptures in the spaces over the doors showed Christ surrounded by the symbols of the four evangelists—the angel of Saint Matthew, the ox of Saint Luke, the eagle of Saint John, and the lion of Saint Mark. The countess entered the church through the center door, which had been opened in her honor. A group of priests stepped forward to greet her and escorted her to a seating area in front of the choir, which sang the Mass. The crowd's sung responses filled the church.

After Mass, the bells rang again. The priests invited Blanche to a small lunch in a room to the side of the altar. The meal consisted of a bit of hot milk sweetened with honey, some bread and butter, a slice of ham, and the plentiful fruits of September. It was a welcome meal, considering the hard day ahead.

The whole week preceding the fair, townspeople saw endless processions of mules loaded with bundles, which were stored in caves dug out of the chalky stone that lay under the city. From the cities of Flanders came huge bolts of draperies, wool, and linen. From even farther away, from Germany and Russia, came furs and leather. The most precious goods were the spices stored in small wooden chests so the flavor would not go flat. The herbs and seasonings brought huge profits to those who traded them. Pepper was the most precious of all, so much so that it was often used as currency. There were also bundles of musk, cinnamon, cloves, cumin, ginger, nutmeg, and sugar. Under the eyes of guards recruited by the city, the merchants set up their stands on the fairgrounds in preparation for the first day of selling.

The opening day of the fair called for an extensive ceremony known as "the clamor of **haro.**" A guard yelled "haro" first, and then the crowd took up the cry in waves. Cries of joy and alarm echoed, as people rushed toward the merchant stands, fearing that everything would disappear before they had had time to buy. The merchants, in excellent humor, moved quickly to satisfy the largest number of customers. The first 12 days of the fair were reserved for draperies and fabrics. The next 8 days were given over to leather and fur.

Spices, however, were traded during the entire fair. Some enhanced the flavor of wines, syrups, and food. Others, like musk, were the basis for perfumes that noblewomen used on themselves and in their homes. Not only were spices the source of great pleasure, people also valued them because they had come from faraway lands.

The clamor of haros finally ended. But the crowd was still noisy as it started milling around. Tavern owners cried out recommendations of their wines, and hawkers sold hot patties, sausages, dried fish, and ready-made sauces for meat. Many jugglers also moved through the crowd, drawing friendly and appreciative audiences. One of them sang a ditty meant to endear himself to the merchants:

Honor the merchants
Above all: they go
By land and sea
To foreign countries
For wool and squirrel fur.
Others sail overseas
To buy spices: pepper,
Cinnamon, and ginger.
God preserve them from harm.

Blanche of Champagne liked the noise and enjoyed the lively crowd. She was glad to see that everything was very orderly. The guards were well placed to catch thieves, particularly purse-snatchers eager to take advantage of the throng. These wrongdoers never took very long making an appearance. Those who were caught stealing money or valuable merchandise were hauled to the **pillory** in the center of the fairgrounds, where their hands were firmly shackled between two solid boards. The offenders would stand there until nightfall so that everyone would know them for what they were.

Blanche and her group did not stay very long at the fair. They had pressing business elsewhere in Provins, particularly at the Palace of the Counts, where she had an appointment with three contractors.

Seven years ago, Roger, Charles, and Pierre had agreed to repair an ancient roadbed that could no longer handle the influx of buyers and sellers at the fairs. The contractors had broadened the road and built two new wooden bridges along the way. They had also paved the road to support the weight of heavy carts. The countess had paid for these improvements by means of tolls that she had allowed the contractors to collect.

On this September day, the three contractors reported that the work, which had been accomplished in sections, was complete. The countess gave her final approval for the job, specifying that from now on the tolls would revert directly to her.

The written agreement was sealed over a hearty meal, washed down with a glass of fine wine. The wine gave Blanche an idea about the rebuilding of the Cathedral of Reims, which had burned down the previous year. Because the church was located within her domain, Blanche of Champagne was in charge of the construction. But before starting on the heavy work—such as excavating the foundations, carting the stone, and raising the scaffolding—she thought it might be a good idea to lay in a supply of wine to encourage the people working on the site. After the meal, Blanche ordered 12 barrels of the same wine to be sent to the workers at the cathedral.

The meal over, Blanche went back to the castle, where she intended to rest. But a messenger had arrived with good news—Thibaut would soon be here! The messenger had ridden hard to inform Blanche, leaving her son behind to proceed at a moderate pace with the rest of the company.

Blanche was filled with joy. Her only son, her beloved son! She had needed much courage to accept a year-long separation. But no doubt the boy had learned many valuable things during his time at the French court. Blanche's happiness knew no bounds. She lay down on a couch that faced the direction where she might see Thibaut and his small escort in the distance. Blanche wondered if she should organize a tournament to honor Thibaut's return or call in some jugglers tonight to entertain him. Wouldn't he be tired after his long journey?

Time passed, and the sun turned west. She saw, far away over the ramparts, something like a cloud of dust. She rose from the couch to be near the window. Yes, it was a group of riders. Maybe it was Thibaut and his escort. With Constance right behind her, Blanche went down the stairs, crossed the guard hall, and settled close to the drawbridge.

Soon the group entered the castle grounds. As they passed by, people held out their hands, applauded, and cried "haro" as they had done at the fair. Within a few moments, a young boy jumped elegantly from his horse, assisted by the royal escort to whom the boy had been entrusted. Thibaut rushed toward his mother, kissed her hand, and then suddenly threw his arms around her.

Mother and son spent long hours together. The child had many things to tell. At the court of France, he had studied. "Do you know what I learned? I know the entire book of Psalms by heart! But I can also read and write!"

He boasted of his riding skills. With the other children at the court, he had learned to handle difficult mounts. He had been taught how to take care of his horse, how to use its equipment, and how to saddle it. He also had learned the game of **quintain.** "You point your lance at a dummy," he said, "but you have to move fast because the dummy pivots and hits you with a club if you are too slow."

He had endless praise for his older cousin from Castile, also named Blanche, who was the wife of the heir to the French crown. The future Louis VIII was nicknamed Louis the Lion, because he had such a short temper.

"And did King Philip treat you well?" Here, Thibaut was not as forthcoming, although he admitted he had certainly been well treated. Yet, to Thibaut, Philip Augustus always seemed to have a lot on his mind. He never spoke much, and even then one never knew if he really meant what he said. The way Thibaut talked, the only person worthy of attention was his cousin Blanche of Castile.

Thibaut thought Blanche of Castile was beautiful, considerate, lighthearted, and full of laughter. She had a quick mind. And she wrote poetry.

"By the way, I also learned to sing and play the **hurdy-gurdy,**" Thibaut added. He showed his mother how he accompanied himself singing.

"During a trip to Languedoc (in south central France), I met Uncle Sancho, who told me things in great confidence," he declared.

Sancho, or King Sancho VII of Navarre, was Blanche's brother. Although Blanche had not seen him for several years, she'd always gotten along well with him.

"Do you know what he told me?," Thibaut continued. "He said that if he stayed childless, he would make me the heir to the kingdom!"

"What a great future you have," said his mother laughing. "You will certainly have a lot on your hands governing Champagne, with its nobles, its merchants, and its fairs, all the things that keep me busy all year. In any event, I hope my brother Sancho has children now that he has married a sister of the count of Toulouse," Blanche added.

While he was giving details about the year spent away from his mother, Thibaut took off his traveling clothes and put on a tunic that his mother had lovingly made.

ventually, the young count and his mother went to dinner. The table was set in the great hall, where the pair sat in the place of honor. Thibaut was happy except for one thing: his cousin Blanche was not there. She obviously had made a tremendous impression. "She is so beautiful with blonde hair, and so sweet!" Thibaut explained. Blanche was amused by his enthusiasm and admiration for his older cousin.

Earlier, Blanche had discreetly sent a **herald** into town to recruit some jugglers to entertain the dinner guests. One of them made a grand entry, leading a bear whose jaws were secured in a leather muzzle. Other jugglers danced with taps on their fingers. What Thibaut enjoyed most, however, was the singer who played a **viol** while reciting a beautiful love poem. Blanche noted how the performance dazzled the boy.

What will this child do with his life, Blanche wondered. Like many people in Champagne, just like his father had wanted to do, he would travel to the Holy Land. Will he be king of Navarre? This was such a distant prospect that she hardly dwelled on it.

But one thing seemed certain: this child was called to be a poet. Although he was only 10 years old, his taste for poetry could not lie. Who could have been happier at this prospect than his mother? Music and poetry had always been her delight. And in the hardest moments of her life, after the death of her beloved husband, they had given her much comfort.

AFTERWORD

In 1234 Thibaut IV did inherit the kingdom of Navarre. He then split his time between his new domain and Champagne, one of the most powerful French counties. In 1284, several decades after Thibaut's death, Champagne's independence ended. In that year, Joan of Navarre—who possessed both Navarre and Champagne—married Philip, the heir to the French throne. Thereafter, the county was considered a royal province and part of the inheritance of French monarchs. In later centuries, war and plague took their toll on the wealth and prosperity of the county. Its position as a major commercial crossroads declined.

The royal takeover of Champagne symbolized a trend within France and other kingdoms. Monarchs were expanding and centralizing their authority by gaining more land—by fair means or by fighting—thereby reducing the power of feudal landowners. By the late 1400s, the feudal system of governing was weakening. Instead of regional centers, such as Champagne, royal courts became the hub of governments.

The rise of central governments in Europe went hand in hand with the growth of trade that had begun in the High Middle Ages. European cities, where wealthy merchants carried on their business, drew people from the countryside. Kings taxed the cities and their inhabitants to fund ambitious royal plans. Meanwhile, the traders and diplomats who traveled throughout Europe became exposed to and then spread new ideas, including a fascination with the ancient civilizations of Greece and Rome. This fascination developed into the Renaissance, or rebirth, of classical studies.

The Roman Catholic Church also came under fire at this time from a movement known as humanism. Rooted in the writings of ancient Greece and Rome, humanism puts great value on human beings and on their central place in nature and society. The Church, on the other hand, had long emphasized its role as the main link between God and Roman Catholics. The medieval Catholic belief—that people were sinful and should work hard to earn heaven—contrasted sharply with the humanistic view that people are good and deserve admiration.

Humanist ideas, including a rejection of rule by a few wealthy families, remained popular long after the Renaissance ended. These ideas had a strong impact on governments that were set up in France and the United States in later centuries.

Glossary

artisan: A person skilled at a certain craft.

cathedral: A church that is the official headquarters of a bishop.

Crusade: One of eight major Christian military expeditions organized in western Europe between 1096 and 1270. The Crusades' stated goal was to recapture Palestine, also called the Holy Land, from Islamic believers called Muslims.

feudalism: The land-based governing system that operated in Europe from the ninth to about the fifteenth centuries.

fief: A feudal estate.

haro: The French cry that opened medieval fairs, for which "hurrah" was the English equivalent.

herald: In medieval times, a person who publicly announced news of common interest to the population, who acted as an official messenger, and who also called together the combatants at tournaments.

hurdy-gurdy: A medieval musical instrument sounded by the friction of a revolving wheel against a set of strings. A crank turned the wheel, while notes were changed by pressing the keys of a small keyboard.

A drawing of a young man picking roses appears in a sixteenth-century edition of the Roman de la Rose, *a long love poem.*

landowner: Under the feudal system, the owner of agricultural land who had power over every aspect of life on the property and made up Europe's ruling class for 400 years. Feudal landowners, in addition to managing their estates, could tax farmers, demand military service, arrange marriages, and impose judicial decisions.

Middle Ages: A period of European history that lasted from roughly A.D. 500 to A.D. 1500. The greatest achievements of the period, known as the **High Middle Ages,** came in the eleventh through the thirteenth centuries.

peasant: A person who tills the soil on land that usually belongs to someone else.

pillory: A wooden frame set on a post with holes for binding the hands and neck. In medieval times and even later, thieves and other wrongdoers were locked in pillories to expose them to public view.

portal: A grand or imposing doorway.

quintain: A revolving dummy set on a pole. Medieval knights, preparing for a tournament or for war, honed their skills by charging the dummy on horseback with a lance. Failure to hit the target squarely in the chest caused the dummy to spin. One of its arms, holding a lance or a heavy bag, would then strike the knight in the back as he rode by. This was also a popular children's game.

rampart: A stone or earthen wall that surrounded a castle, fortress, or fortified city for purposes of defense.

regent: A person, usually a relative, who governs a kingdom while the actual ruler is too young, is too sick, or is out of the kingdom.

Renaissance: A period of European history that followed the Middle Ages and blended into the modern era.

Roman Catholic Church: A Christian religious organization that was founded in the late Roman Empire. After the empire's fall in the fifth century A.D., chaos followed. The Catholic Church became the main source of leadership, political power, and education until the feudal system evolved in the ninth century.

serf: A low-ranking, unpaid member of feudal society bound to the estate of a lord and subject to his will.

squire: A knight's servant. During the Middle Ages, young men who aspired to become knights would first become squires to learn the skills of knighthood from the knights they served. In a wider sense, squires could also be in the personal service of a lady with the specific task of caring for horses and arms.

viol: A medieval stringed instrument played with a bow that was the ancestor of the fiddle.

ward: An underage person who is under the protection and authority of another.

A drawing from the thirteenth century depicts a lady with her dog and a bird of prey.

PRONUNCIATION GUIDE

Aube	OHB
Blanche	BLA^{N}SH
Champagne	sham-PAH^{N}
Ecry-sur-Aisne	eh-cree–soor–AYN
feudalism	FYOO-duhl-ih-zehm
fief	FEEF
Foulques	FOOLK
haro	ah-ROH
Lagny	lah^{n}-YEE
Languedoc	la^{n}-guh-DAHK
medieval	mee-DEE-vuhl
Marne	MAHRN
Navarre	nah-VAHR
Neuilly	nuh-YEE
Provins	proh-VAA^{N}
quintain	KWIN-tehn
Reims	RAA^{N}S
Renaissance	REHN-uh-sahns
Saint Ayoul	SAA^{N} aye-YOOL
Seine	SAYNE
Sens	SAH^{N}S
Thibaut	TEE-BOH
Troyes	truh-WAH

FURTHER READING LIST

Arnold, Caroline. *Juggler.* New York: Clarion Books, 1988.

Clements, Gillian. *The Truth About Castles.* Minneapolis: Carolrhoda Books, Inc., 1988.

Corbin, Carole Lynn. *Knights.* New York: Franklin Watts, 1989.

France in Pictures. Minneapolis: Lerner Publications Company, Geography Department, 1991.

Ganeri, Anita. *Focus on France and the French.* New York: Gloucester Press, 1992.

Gravett, Christopher. *Castle.* New York: Alfred A. Knopf, 1994.

Hills, Ken. *Crusades.* New York: Marshall Cavendish, 1991.

Howarth, Sarah. *Medieval People.* Brookfield, CT: The Millbrook Press, 1992.

Howarth, Sarah. *Medieval Places.* Brookfield, CT: The Millbrook Press, 1992.

Langley, Andrew. *Medieval Life.* New York: Alfred A. Knopf, 1996.

Macdonald, Fiona. *A Medieval Castle.* New York: Peter Bedrick Books, Inc., 1993.

Stewart, Gail B. *Life on a Medieval Pilgrimage.* San Diego: Lucent Books, 1996.

Williams, Brian. *Forts and Castles.* New York: Penguin, 1995.

INDEX

ABOUT THE
AUTHOR AND THE ILLUSTRATOR

Régine Pernoud, an internationally known expert on life in the Middle Ages, studied at L'Ecole de Chartres and L'Ecole du Louvre before becoming curator successively of the Museum of Reims in Reims, the Museum of the History of France at the National Archives in Paris, and the Joan of Arc Center in Orléans. A resident of Paris, Ms. Pernoud is the author of more than 40 scholarly works translated into many languages.

Giorgio Bacchin, a native of Milan, Italy, studied the graphic arts in his hometown. After years of freelance graphic design, Mr. Bacchin has completely devoted himself to book illustration. His works have appeared in educational and trade publications.